Truly Beautiful

A Word from the Author

It's God who sees the beauty in everything, I just choose to agree with Him.

Sweet Pea - Veggie Tales

Sweet Pea got it right; she chose to agree with God! My prayer for you as you journey through the next ten weeks in this study is that you will agree with Sweet Pea and see yourself the way God sees you.

Every day as you awake and stare into the mirror of God's Word, you will discover just how "truly beautiful" you are and that your Creator made you beautiful for HIM!

As a writer, author and biblical counselor, my heart is often stirred to teach on what I see coming through my counseling sessions. God called me to write this study as I witnessed many young women suffering from a lack of understanding of who they are in Christ.

Jesus often used the word "truly" to preface profound biblical truths He wanted us grasp. I can't think of anything that is more crucial to the foundation of a young Christian woman's life as her position in Christ. She must know that she is not just "beautiful" but "Truly Beautiful."

It has been said the Christian life is the becoming of "who you are" in Christ. My desire is that God would use this study in your life to help you embrace and live in the reality that you are His masterpiece. My hope is that you would trust Him and walk confidently into the unique purpose and plan He has designed just for you.

Praying for you!

Margy Hill

Study Lessons

Week One

Defining the Beauty Battle

You Are My True Beauty

Your real beauty is a work of art, hand carved by Me.

I have given you beautiful lips to speak words of life, beautiful eyes to see Me in everything, beautiful hands to help those in need, and a beautiful face to reflect My love to the world. I know you don't see yourself the way I do, because you compare yourself to beauty idols that will soon be forgotten.

I will work wonders that will radiate true beauty from within. And when my work is completed, your character will show off my craftsmanship, and your beauty marks will be remembered by all that were loved by you.

Love,

Your Radiant King

Sheri Rose Shepherd

This Week's Focus

Defining the Beauty Battle

The Enemy of Beauty

For many young women today, embracing your God-given beauty and value is a life long struggle. There is a longing deep within you to fit in; to be accepted, and to be beautiful. Your generation is bombarded daily with billboards, fashion magazines and media that generate false messages about beauty. But because the battle with beauty goes deeper than what your eye can see, you are susceptible to the lies that come against what it means to be, "truly beautiful".

Who is behind the lies about beauty?

- Is it the culture?
- Is it the airbrushed supermodels and the fashion industry?
- Is it the billion dollar diet craze and plastic surgery phenomena?

Though these influences contribute to the fight, we must recognize our real enemy.

His name is Satan.

What does Satan gain by attacking our perception of beauty and worth?

Those answers can be found in God's Word with a little bit of history on Satan. He is no stranger to the allure of beauty; in fact, Ezekiel describes him as "perfect in beauty". But that beauty became his downfall and the consequences of his pride got him thrown out of heaven. His splendor led to rebellion and he has been wreaking havoc ever since. His goal is to destroy the image of God in us and he ruthlessly seeks to come against women to twist and pervert the truths about beauty.

You need only look at the outer ravaged body of a young woman with anorexia to know that the lies she has believed in her heart are destroying her. Or, the young woman who has scars all over her body, from the cuts of a razor blade, that were meant to dull the inner pain she could not handle.

Satan knows all too well that if he gets a young woman to buy into the lies about beauty, she will soon find herself disappointed, depressed and eventually destroyed. For this reason it is important that you discover God's truth. That you see yourself as God sees you, for it is in His truth that you come to know and believe that you are "truly beautiful".

Beauty Truth #1 = to be truly beautiful is to see yourself as God sees you.

Applying this truth to my life

Read Ezekiel 28:11-17. Though the passage is referring to the King of Tyre, the Scripture is also speaking to the evil one working in his life. God is giving us a picture of Satan and his fall from the garden.

1. We quickly see the sins of **PRIDE**, **LUST** and **IDOLATRY** are all intertwined in the beauty battle. Define these words and give a current example of how we see these sins working themselves out in beautiful young women today.

2. What are some of the **false** promises of physical beauty? Fill in the blank.

   • If you're beautiful, you will be_____

   • If you're beautiful, you will be_____

   • If you're beautiful, you will be_____

   • If you're beautiful, you will be_____

   • If you're beautiful, you will be_____

   • If you're beautiful, you will be_____

3. Have you **fallen** for some of these false promises of beauty? Describe your experience.

An Identity Crisis

Dictionary.com defines the word **identity** as; *the fact of being who, or what a person or thing is*. Simply put, identity is **who we are**. Christian rap artist Lecrae got it right when he wrote:

> *Identity is found in the God we trust*
> *Any other identity will self-destruct*

God created us in His image and we were made to find our identity in Him. As we enter into a personal relationship with His Son, Jesus, we become children of God and we are then able to walk in the amazing plan and purpose that we were created for, a life with value and significance that brings glory to our Creator.

We must be able to spot the **identity** lies of our culture. The root of these lies comes as the thief, Satan, seeks to tempt us to find our identity in our physical appearance.

Jesus is clear to present the way of truth versus the way of lies in John 10:10:

> *The thief does not come except to steal, and to kill, and to destroy.*
> *I have come that they may have life, and that they may have it more abundantly.*

Our identity is found in the God who created us, any other identity ***will self-destruct***. Why - because the beauty battle is a battle against everything that is good, true, right and beautiful. Our enemy Satan, who was prideful in his beauty, went against God. His anger and fury rages on to pervert and destroy God's image in women. Trying to find our identity in the **outer** beauty the world sells will leave a woman empty, disappointed and wounded every time.

Place your trust in the One, Who calls you His masterpiece, the One who has an exciting purpose and plan for your life, the One who loves you with an everlasting love, and the One who has nothing but your best interest at heart. Though the battle continues, you can have a peace in the midst of it as you come to discover the truth of who you were really meant to be.

> *I'm not the shoes I wear*
> *I'm not the clothes I buy*
> *I'm am not the house I live in*
> *I'm not the car I drive*
> *I'm not the job I work*
> *You can't define my worth*
> *By nothing on God's green earth*
> *My identity is found in Christ.*

> Lecrae

Beauty Truth #2 = to be truly beautiful is to know that your identity is found in the God who created you.

Applying this truth to my life

1. Movies, magazines, and music, how do they affect the way you think about beauty?

2. How does what you see in the media contrast with what God's Word says about women and beauty?

3. Why is it important that you seek to find your identity in the Word of God versus trying to find it out in the culture?

Beauty: To What Extreme

Have you ever watched the final tear jerking moments of Extreme Makeover, and felt a bit envious? A woman completely transformed on the outside reveals her new **identity** as she walks into a room full of amazed family and friends! Though there is a radical makeover on the **outside**, will it take care of what troubles her on the **inside**?

Physical beauty doesn't ensure happiness, fulfillment, or success. We see the downward spiral of many young women in Hollywood believing the lie that beauty will bring happiness. The Hollywood lifestyle quickly takes its toll. It is not long before they find themselves used up and made fools of on some reality show. They are demeaned by the very fans that cheered for them in the beginning. Their outward beauty quickly fades as they succumb to the ugliness of the lies they have believed in their heart.

Beauty Truth #3 = to be truly beautiful is to recognize our desire for beauty can result in the sin of pride and selfishness.

Let's Talk About It

Miley Cyrus caused a stir with parents in 2010 when she appeared in a highly provocative music video launching her song, <u>Who Owns My Heart</u>. The lyrics reveal her personal struggle with lies about beauty:

I want to believe I'm a masterpiece, but sometimes it's hard in the dark

The lies about beauty are dark, and they take us to dark places.

- Who owns your heart?

- Why is it so important that God and His Word rule and reign in your heart?

Week Two

Winning the Beauty Battle

This Week's Focus

Winning the Beauty Battle

It is wonderful to know that God has provided the necessary principles that will help you to walk in victory as you fight your way through the beauty battle. There are **4** great truths we want to embrace in God's Word that build a strong foundation in a young woman's life as she seeks to make wise choices and decisions regarding beauty.

BEAUTY PRINCIPLES

1

Recognize that your body does not belong to you, but to God. Your body was meant to glorify Him, to be a living sacrifice, so any time you consider your body and how to treat it, you must consult the Owner.
1 Corinthians 6:19-20

2

With a focus on pleasing God, you can make confident choices concerning your appearance. With your identity being anchored in Christ, you can walk in a balanced approach to taking care of yourself and avoid the wrong thinking that tempts you to see beauty as a way to gain worth and value.
Ephesians 1:6

3

God graciously allows you the freedom in Christ to make personal choices, but you are expected to make wise and godly decisions that will distinguish you from the rest of the world. Your freedoms are never to be used in a way that will tarnish your Christian testimony.
1 Peter 1:15

4

Your focus should be on your inner woman. God is looking at your heart. There is nothing wrong with taking care of your outward appearance but when it becomes the issue that drives you, that consumes all of your thinking, time and money; be sure to check your heart and your priorities.
1 Peter 3:4

BEAUTY TRUTH #4 - to be truly beautiful is to embrace a biblical beauty perspective.

Applying this truth to my life

Your greatest source of beauty is a thriving and fruitful relationship with Jesus Christ. A daily diet of His Word and abiding in His presence will change you from the inside out. The beauty that is in your heart will make its way to a glow on the outside that will turn heads wherever you go.

1. How can nurturing your **inner** beauty benefit your **outward** beauty?

2. Look up the following verses and discover some of the biblical beauty products you can apply to be "truly beautiful".

   - Cleanser (1 John 1:9)

   - Foundation (Psalm 119:11)

   - Blush (Matthew 5:16)

   - Lipstick (Proverbs 16:24)

3. Where do you need victory in the beauty battle? What are some truths from God's Word that can help you to fight back?

Beauty and the Book of Ephesians

Tucked away in the Book of Ephesians, Chapter 2, verse 10, is the most beautiful description of a believer in all of Scripture:

For we are God's masterpiece.
He has created us anew in Christ Jesus,
so we can do the good things he planned for us long ago. (NLT)

The treasures of Ephesians center on the truth that **YOU** are God's masterpiece. What is a masterpiece? It is the deepest expression of the artist! When you listen to a beautiful song, or set your eyes on a beautiful painting, what you're hearing, or what you're seeing, is the deepest expression of who that person is.

And here's the thing that is absolutely awesome about what Paul is saying here: you are God's deepest expression. God wants to express Himself, like any other artist would do through their art. You are God's art. You're God's masterpiece. And what does He want to do with you? He wants to express Himself through you.

Fill in the blanks with some words that you would use to describe a masterpiece.

- A masterpiece is_____

- A masterpiece is_____

- A masterpiece is_____

- A masterpiece is_____

- A masterpiece is_____

- A masterpiece is_____

- A masterpiece is_____

- A masterpiece is_____

- A masterpiece is_____

BEAUTY TRUTH #5 – to be truly beautiful is to discover who I am in Christ and appropriate those truths in my life.

Applying this truth to my life

1. Some of Paul's most powerful prayers are found in the Book of Ephesians. Read Ephesians 1:15-21 and 3:14-21. What is Paul praying that you would embrace and live out in your life?

2. God created you with real desires. There are **4** which you will be looking at throughout your study:

   - *The desire to know lasting intimacy and true love*

   - *The desire to be confident, secure and accepted*

   - *The desire to live a life that is meaningful and significant*

   - *The desire to be whole and holy*

Though our desires our valid, they were meant to be satisfied and fulfilled by God. Unless a young woman understands who she is in Christ and how to practically live out those truths, she will seek to fulfill her real needs in the wrong way.

Give some examples of how young women seek to fulfill real needs in the wrong way.

Week 3

Daddy's Girl

You Are My Precious Daughter

You are a daughter of the King, and not just any king.

You are My daughter, and I am the God of all heaven and earth. I'm delighted with you! You are the apple of my eye. You're Daddy's girl. Your earthly father may love and adore you, but his love is not perfect, no matter how great, or small, it is. Only My love is perfect because I am love. I formed your body. I fashioned your mind and soul. I know your personality, and I understand your needs and desires. I see your heartaches and disappointments, and I love you passionately and patiently. My child, I bought you with a price so that we could have an intimate relationship together for all eternity. Soon we will see each other face to face, Father and daughter, and you will experience the wonderful place I have prepared for you in paradise. Until then, fix your eyes on heaven, and walk closely with Me. You will know that, although I am God, My arms are not too big to hold you, my beloved daughter.

Love,

Your King and your Daddy

in Heaven

Sheri Rose Shepherd

This Week's Focus

Daddy's Girl

Read Ephesians 1:3-6.

Blessed be the God and Father of our Lord Jesus Christ, who has blessed us with every spiritual blessing in the heavenly places in Christ, just as He chose us in Him before the foundation of the world, that we should be holy and without blame before Him in love, having predestined us to adoption as sons by Jesus Christ to Himself, according to the good pleasure of His will, to the praise of the glory of His grace, by which He made us accepted in the Beloved.

The Father Longing

The supreme revelation of God in the Bible is that He is your Father. The key to knowing you are "truly beautiful" is that you are Daddy's girl! Eight times in the Book of Ephesians we are told about our Father. It is a relationship we want to live out and enjoy each and every day. God, your Father, has blessed you with every spiritual blessing in Christ to live in the heavenlies; this is a place where you are able to rise above the struggles of every day life.

In 1997 singer and songwriter Bob Carlisle wrote a beautiful ballad called, "Butterfly Kisses". The song describes the tender love between a father and his daughter. The song rose to the top of the charts quickly. In reflecting upon the song's enormous success, Bob Carlisle said this:

I get a lot of mail from young girls who try to get me to marry their moms. That used to be a real chuckle because it's so cute, but then I realized they don't want a romance for Mom. They want the father that is in that song, and that just kills me.

What these young girls wanted was a daddy; a dad to love them, a dad to protect them, a dad to be kind and tender toward them. They wanted a dad who is strong, dependable and committed, a dad to help them along the way as they grew up, a dad to guide them, a dad to be their greatest fan.

This same longing is reminiscent of the longing that resides in each of our hearts, to be Daddy's little girl. God has created within our hearts a longing to be fathered by the Father of our dreams, our perfect heavenly Father. The need to be well fathered is a fundamental need of the human heart. It is a need that was put in us by our Creator, the heavenly Father, and our true Father, Who alone defines what fatherhood means and what fatherhood was meant to be.

BEAUTY TRUTH #6 = to be truly beautiful is to know lasting intimacy and acceptance rests in your relationship to God as your Father.

Applying this truth to my life

1. Look up three scriptures that speak to God's love for you.

2. Look up the following scriptures and record what you discover about your heavenly Father.

   • Psalm 56:8

   • Isaiah 49:16

   • Matthew 10:30

3. Read the story of the prodigal son in Luke 15:11-32. Write down everything you learn about his father.

Let's Talk About It

Have you been running away from God? Even now, the Father's heart is turned toward you. His arms are outstretched waiting for you to return to safety and the comfort of His love. Will you turn your heart toward Him? Why or why not?

Journal

Sometimes we can make the mistake of thinking that our heavenly Father is like our earthly father. Even the best father can not compare to your perfect Father. Take some time to journal about the kind of relationship you have or wished you had with your father.

Daughter

In Mark chapter 5:25-34, we read about a woman who suffered with an issue of blood for 12 years. Imagine her life, rejected and alone. Society had shunned her and labeled her unclean. She had wasted all of her time, energy and money seeking her healing from the world, which left her not better, only worse.

In a moment of complete and utter despair, desperate to be healed, she reaches out with great faith to touch the hem of Jesus' garment. Immediately we are told the fountain of her blood is dried up and she felt in her body that she was healed of the affliction. But that is not the end of the story. Jesus calls her out by asking a question He already had the answer to, "Who touched my clothes"? With fear and trembling she comes out from the crowd falling down before Jesus, sharing the truth of her life with Him.

There was probably much sin to confess as a result of the very real pain and agony she had suffered over those twelve long years. What happens next is crucial to our study. Jesus responds:

> *Daughter, your faith has made you well. Go in peace, and be healed of your affliction.*

DAUGHTER. This endearing, affectionate term, signified her new relationship with Jesus. Her faith had caused her to come to Jesus, to confess to Him, and He healed her physically and spiritually.

She had placed her trust in Jesus and now became a daughter, adopted into the family, no longer rejected but accepted in the Beloved. We become a daughter of God by faith in His Son, Jesus. We then enjoy a personal relationship with the Creator of the universe! That means we can get to know Him. It means we can talk to Him and relate to Him on an intimate basis. We may not completely understand how to relate to an Almighty One, or the Most High, or the Great I Am, because we have no earthly frame of reference to do so, but relating to a father, that's different!

Write out some words that describe your idea of the perfect father.

- The perfect father is_____

- The perfect father is_____

- The perfect father is_____

- The perfect father is_____

- The perfect father is_____

- The perfect father is_____

BEAUTY TRUTH #7 – to be truly beautiful is to know that you are God's daughter.

Apply it to Your Life

1. At the root of much of a young woman's depression, her self-loathing, and sometimes her hopelessness and despair, is the lie that God could not possibly love her. Why is it so important that we come to grow in the understanding of God's love for us?

2. How do we nourish an intimate relationship with God? What things can hinder that intimacy? Use Scripture to support your answer.

3. Take some time to write a love letter to your Heavenly Father.

Week 4

Chosen for Relationship

This Week's Focus

Chosen for Relationship

God always takes the initiative in our love relationship. The witness of the entire Bible testifies that God pursues us, that He chose us before the foundation of the world to have a relationship with Him. What does it mean to be chosen? Webster Dictionary defines it this way:

Selected or marked for favor or special privilege
Or one who is the object of choice or divine favor

Many a young woman has dreaded those times during P.E. when the team captains were given the opportunity to choose their team members. What a nerve-wracking moment when one by one the more popular girls were picked while the less popular girls prayed they would not be the last one chosen!

God chose you! Let that sink in. GOD CHOSE YOU. He tore Himself away from heaven to come and be with you, the one He loves and chose to be His own to accomplish His purposes in this generation. Before the foundation of the world God had a plan to bring you to Him.

You can have joy, assurance and peace in knowing that God predestined you to be adopted as His child for all eternity and He did this before you were even born! It was His will, His love and great pleasure to choose you!

When you begin to see yourself in the hands of a Father who loved you and chose you personally, it will revolutionize your life. Your fear of rejection is won by your faith in His unfailing love and His promise to never leave or forsake you.

It was Charles Spurgeon who commented:

Nothing under the gracious influence of the Holy Spirit can make a Christian more holy than the thought that she is chosen. Shall I sin, she says, after God has chosen me? Shall I transgress after such love? Shall I go astray after so much loving kindness and tender mercy?

Let's Talk About It

Share a time when you experienced rejection. How does it encourage you to know that God will never reject you?

Beauty Truth #8 = to be truly beautiful is to live in the joy and excitement of being chosen by God.

1. What do you discover you were chosen for in John 15:16?

2. Continue to search the Scriptures and describe what the Word is revealing to you about being chosen.

   - Deuteronomy 7:6-8

   - Deuteronomy 14:2

   - Ephesians 1:4

   - 2 Thessalonians 2:13

   - 1 Peter 2:9-10

3. What does it mean to you to be chosen by God?

Abba

Did you know that the Holy Spirit that lives in you is continually crying out Abba, or Daddy? Under the influence of the Holy Spirit, your whole being, heart, mind, soul and strength cries out with an intense longing to connect with your Father.

There is a strong and desperate desire for lasting intimacy that calls us and drives us to the Father's heart. Often we don't recognize the longing. We can't explain why we feel restless or frustrated. Busyness disguises the pain and disappointment we seek to keep under control. We attempt to satisfy our yearnings with substitutes that leave us continually empty. We go about life on our own forgetting the One who is ready and waiting to fill us with His love and comfort.

It is so important that we recognize the yearnings in our heart when they come, so that we will turn to the One who can satisfy those longings. Are you going ever deeper in your relationship with God? Are you confidently and joyfully entering into His presence? Do you experience His love for you as His daughter? In the difficult times, who do you cry out to?

Intimacy is established in our Father-daughter relationship when we share all of our lives with God. He wants us to run to Him and crawl up in His lap and linger there, to be honest about our sin and share our fears. He longs to bring comfort and healing and address the deep hurts and pains we try to avoid. Our deepest desire for lasting intimacy will be completely fulfilled when we are finally at home, with our perfect heavenly Father for all of eternity.

Beauty Truth #9 = to be truly beautiful is to recognize my desire for intimacy is only fulfilled in my relationship with God my Father.

Apply it to Your Life

1. Write out Romans 8:15.

2. Who or what do you reach out to when your heart is longing for relationship?

3. Look up the word **abide** in a Bible dictionary. How does the definition help you to better understand the idea of an intimate relationship with God?

Accepted in the Beloved

Every little girl loves to play dress-up. Give her a plastic crown, a pink tutu and a wand and she will instantly become a princess. Likewise, give a little boy a cap and badge and he will immediately become a police officer. We smile at a child's role playing, but how much do we play dress-up in real life? How often do we pretend to be something or somebody that we really are not?

- *We want to belong or be accepted so we dress and act like those we hope will include us.*

- *We pretend to have interest in things in which we have no interest in order to impress or attract someone.*

- *We do things we don't want to do just so we can conform to a certain image or expectation.*

In addition, we often hide or mask our true thoughts and feelings. We may laugh when we feel like crying, act fearless when we are scared to death, and act like we have it altogether when we're falling apart.

Why do we feel the need to be someone different from who we really are? Why do we feel that we cannot be honest about our true thoughts and feelings? Often it is because of fear. We want to be liked and accepted so it is difficult to be totally, completely honest with others. We fear people won't like us if they really know us, our weaknesses, insecurities, doubts, and frustrations. It seems easier to pretend to be the person we think they want us to be.

Isn't it wonderful to know that God accepts you just the way you are, whether you have it all together or you fail miserably? Did you know that He sees you completed and in glory? When He looks at you He sees you covered by the blood of Christ.
God is not counting your sins, but looking for the opportunities that you choose to believe Him. Your sins are paid for, ***past, present and future***! To God you are the praise of His glory and it is His good pleasure to accept you into the Beloved.

It was God's plan that the Lord Jesus would give His life for you at Calvary by dying on the cross. When you recognized your need for Jesus, confessed your sin, and trusted Him with your life, God now sees you in the Beloved. His Spirit now lives inside you to give you the power to live for Him.

Beauty Truth #10 = to be truly beautiful is to be accepted in the Beloved.

Apply it to Your Life

God now sees you in the Beloved, to the praise and glory of His grace. God's glory is greatly enhanced by the grace He has shown to us. We love God because He first loved us. It was God, your Heavenly Father's plan to seek you out, to save you, to sanctify you and seat you in glory.

1. Write out the words of 1 John 4:19.

2. *You cannot hide from God or pretend to be something you're not because He knows you perfectly.* Read Psalm 139:1-16 and write out the things that God knows about you.

3. You never need to worry that God will stop loving you. What does He promise you in Romans 8:38-39?

Read the poem below and journal your thoughts.

Father, You see me as I am,
You know me through and through,
There's nothing within or without
That I can hide from You.
Father, such knowledge comforts me,
For I don't need to pretend,
I can be honest and open with You,
You'll always be my friend.

You see beyond my armor,
The thick shell I hide within,
And You peel away each layer,
To let Your light shine in.
You soften all the hard spots,
The roughened edges, You smooth,
You give purpose and direction,
My tumultuous heart, You soothe.

You transform this misfit,
Who did not fit in before,
And You give me life and victory,
I'm not a misfit anymore.

Journal your thoughts

Pause & Pray

Your Heavenly Father created you to have a relationship with Him. He loves you and longs for you to be His daughter. Your sins have separated you from Him and can not be removed by your good deeds. Jesus paid the price for your sins on the cross. He died and rose again. Everyone who trusts and places their faith in Jesus alone has eternal life. Once your decision is made, your life with Jesus starts at that moment and lasts forever.

If you have not yet entered into a personal relationship with God, by placing your faith in His Son, Jesus Christ, take a moment now to pray and confess your need for Him. Be sure to let another believer know about your decision and ask them to help you learn how to live for Him!

G O D created us to be with Him.

O U R sins separate us from God.

S I N S cannot be removed by good deeds.

P AY I N G the price for sin, Jesus died and rose again.

E V E R Y O N E who trusts in Him alone has eternal life.

L I F E with Jesus starts now and lasts forever.

If you placed your trust in Jesus today, write the date below, so you can always remember your spiritual birthday. If you received Jesus prior to the study, write the date you were saved.

_____

30

Week 5

The Search for True Love

My Princess I will protect you

I am your shield of protection.

Many times you wonder where I am in the midst of the battle that rages around you. You feel abandoned on the battlefield. Don't be afraid and don't lose faith. I am here, and I am always victorious. I will protect you, but you must trust Me. Sometimes I will lead you to shelter for safety and restoration. Other times I will ask you to join Me on the front line in the heat of the battle. The truth is, I can kill any giant that threatens your life, but, just like David the shepherd boy, it's up to you to march forward, pick up the stones, and face your giant.

I love to prove My strength when the odds are the greatest and hope is smallest. I am truly your Shelter and your Deliverer, I will protect you no matter where you are.

Love,

Your King and Protector

Sheri Rose Shepherd

This Week's Focus

The Search for True Love

Read Ephesians 2:1-10.

And you He made alive, who were dead in trespasses and sins, in which you once walked according to the course of this world, according to the prince of the power of the air, the spirit who now works in the sons of disobedience, among whom also we all once conducted ourselves in the lusts of our flesh, fulfilling the desires of the flesh and of the mind, and were by nature children of wrath, just as the others. But God, who is rich in mercy, because of His great love with which He loved us, even when we were dead in trespasses, made us alive together with Christ (by grace you have been saved), and raised us up together, and made us sit together in the heavenly places in Christ Jesus, that in the ages to come He might show the exceeding riches of His grace in His kindness toward us in Christ Jesus. For by grace you have been saved through faith, and that not of yourselves; it is the gift of God, not of works, lest anyone should boast. For we are His workmanship, created in Christ Jesus for good works, which God prepared beforehand that we should walk in them.

Rich in Grace

What are the dimensions of the grace of God? How extensive are the resources of His grace? So often we drastically underestimate the measure of God's supply of grace for our lives like a little fish thinking the ocean may not be large enough for him.

Yet, in delivering us by His grace He did not deplete the treasures of His grace. In Ephesians 2:7, God speaks of the "exceeding riches of His grace." The Lord's grace is far beyond any richness that we have ever yet comprehended or experienced. God's storehouse of grace is so abundantly full that He will be pouring it out upon us for the "ages to come." Yes, it will take eternity for the Lord to fully demonstrate His grace toward us. This everlasting demonstration of His grace will involve showing His kindness toward all of us who are in Christ Jesus. The dimensions of God's grace are sufficient for Him to make us the objects of His kindness forever and ever!

God's grace is like an infinitely vast ocean. Think of the immensity of the oceans of the world. Although they are magnificent in scope, every ocean can be searched out or understood. Every ocean has a bottom that can be reached. Though vast, they are finite. Paul testified that the Lord gave him grace to go forth and proclaim the "unsearchable (unfathomable) riches of Christ." There is more grace available in the heart of God for us than there is water in all of the oceans of the world! Truly, no matter how much grace we have already discovered in Christ, we have only begun to search out the riches of His grace toward us. Thus, Peter admonishes us to "grow in grace" and in the knowledge of our Lord and Savior Jesus Christ. So swim "little fish" and explore as much as possible the ocean of "the riches of His grace."

GRACE = God's Riches At Christ's Expense!

33

Beauty Truth #11 - to be truly beautiful is to know and live in the riches of God's grace.

Apply it to Your Life

1. Look up the word **grace** in a bible dictionary or concordance and write out some definitions.

2. How has God's grace worked in your life and how is it continuing to work in your life?

3. How does God's grace enable us to extend grace to others?

4. Why is grace so important to the Christian life? Use Scripture to support your answer.

5. Share your favorite scripture on grace.

The Beauty of Brokenness

Our generation has been programmed to pursue happiness, good feelings about ourselves, and a positive self-image. But God is not as interested in these ends as we are. He is more committed to making us holy than making us happy. And there is only one pathway to holiness, one road to genuine revival, and that is the pathway of humility or brokenness.

At first hearing, **brokenness** does not sound like something to be sought after. After all, it seems so negative! We may even be afraid of the concept. Perhaps that is because we have a misconception about the meaning of brokenness. Our idea may be quite different from God's idea. Let me provide you with a definition that I think will help you to better understand it.

Brokenness is that place where we realize that all the things we counted on to make life work, don't. God makes life work. Brokenness often happens when we've crossed over the line of what we can handle on our own, leaving us with nowhere to turn.

Brokenness is a lifestyle of agreeing with God about the true condition of my heart and life, as He sees it. It is a lifestyle of unconditional, absolute surrender of my will to the will of God, a heart attitude that says, "Yes, Lord!" to whatever God says. Brokenness means the shattering of my self-will, so that the life and Spirit of the Lord Jesus may be released through me.

BEAUTY TRUTH #12 - To be truly beautiful is a lifestyle of agreeing with God about the true condition of my heart and life, as He sees it.

Apply it to Your Life

1. Read Psalm 34:18 and Isaiah 57:15. How do they help you to better understand what you are learning about brokenness?

2. Brokenness is my response of humility and obedience to the conviction of the Word and the Spirit of God. As my conviction is continuous, so must my brokenness be continuous. Why is it important that we come to the Word of God with an **attitude of brokenness?** Use Scripture to support your answer.

3. God allows defeat, setback, adversity, or tragedy to bring us to the end of self. In the process He makes us more and more like Christ. What is God allowing in your life right now to bring you to the end of self? Are you cooperating or resisting?

4. True spiritual brokenness is a reflection of a life given to humility and a contrite spirit. Real brokenness is reflected in the young woman who acknowledges she is no longer her own, she has been bought with a price. Such a woman yields herself to God to be broken and formed into the image of Christ. What are some ways you can develop a lifestyle of brokenness?

Let's Talk About It

In our minds broken things lose their value. But God doesn't toss aside broken things. He values them. They are priceless. He remakes them and uses them for His glory. When we are broken, we give to God that which the world views as worthless, and He makes it priceless. You are a trophy of God's grace!

Share a moment of brokenness in your life and how God used it for His glory.

True Love

Ecclesiastes 3:11 tells us that God has made everything beautiful in its time, that He has put eternity in our hearts except that no one can find out the work that God does from beginning to end. He is making us perfectly beautiful. Not one stroke of His hand is out of place or wrong, *it is all beautiful*. He has placed the desire for true love in our hearts and it is Him and only Him that will fulfill our deepest longings.

1 Corinthians 13 tells us that God's love suffers long and He is kind. He thinks no evil toward you. He is unfailing in His love for you. His love is not imperfect or evil like man's love but perfect. Do you know that God loves you with a perfect love?

We often buy into the lie that God is just like us. He is not! God is good, perfectly good and His plans are good; they are to prosper you and not to harm you, to give you a hope and a future. If we believed God's love was true, we would not keep returning to a worldly love, only to be disappointed time and time again. We must allow ourselves to bask in God's grace, recognizing at all times our complete and utter need for Him. We must trust His perfect love instead of reaching out for cheap substitutes.

These substitutes will leave us disappointed every time. We need to trust the One who created us; the One who knows the beginning from the end, the One who loves us perfectly.

Take some time to identify the cheap substitutes you are tempted to reach out to, instead of reaching out for God's perfect love.

SUBSTITUTES FOR GOD'S LOVE

- When I am lonely, I reach out to_____

- When I am feeling unloved, I reach out to_____

- When I am sad, I reach out to_____

- When I am disappointed, I reach out to_____

- When I am angry, I reach out to_____

BEAUTY TRUTH #13 - to be truly beautiful is to trust the One who loves you perfectly.

Apply it to Your Life

1. Why do you think it is so hard to trust God with your life?

2. What person or circumstance are you having a hard time trusting God for right now?

3. Read 1 Corinthians 13:4-8(a) from the Message paraphrase and underline or highlight what you most appreciate about God's love for you.

> *Love never gives up.*
> *Love cares more for others than for self.*
> *Love doesn't want what it doesn't have.*
> *Love doesn't strut,*
> *Doesn't have a swelled head,*
> *Doesn't force itself on others,*
> *Isn't always "me first,"*
> *Doesn't fly off the handle,*
> *Doesn't keep score of the sins of others,*
> *Doesn't revel when others grovel,*
> *Takes pleasure in the flowering of truth,*
> *Puts up with anything,*
> *Trusts God always,*
> *Always looks for the best,*
> *Never looks back,*
> *But keeps going to the end.*

4. What can you do to embrace God's love in your life?

Week 6

My Prince Charming

Where is My Prince Charming?

In the fairy tale the beautiful princess always ended up with Prince Charming. Well, what about everybody else? This question cuts deeply to tender, fragile and emotional issues of the heart.

Some of you reading thought you had found that one special relationship. You hoped for it and invested your heart in it only to be disappointed as you watched it crumble in a heap of unfulfilled expectations and broken dreams. The fact is, that in human relationships, there are few guarantees. They will always have their disappointments, days of regret, and loneliness. Such is the danger of relationships in a fallen world.

But we do see in the Bible promises that lead us to believe that we can trust God to fulfill the deeper need we have for companionship, that of knowing and being known fully by Him.

Remember that while no one can know you completely, God knows everything about you and loves you anyway. He accepts you just the way you are and He wants to be with you now and forever. He will never abandon you and He is able to meet all of your needs. He is the one special relationship you have been dreaming of all along that will never sour and never disappoint.

As for the beautiful princess that always gets Prince Charming, you are that beautiful princess and you have Jesus to thank for that. He is your Prince Charming and the book of Revelation tells us He will come as your Hero to save the day riding on a white horse!

BEAUTY TRUTH #14 - to be truly beautiful is to know that you are a beautiful princess and Jesus is your Prince Charming.

Apply it to Your Life

1. Read Romans 5:8. How did God demonstrate His love towards you?

2. Read Revelation 19:11-16. How should the fact that Jesus is both **faithful** and **true** impact the way you live?

Write a letter of gratitude to your *Prince Charming* for coming to your rescue!

Dear Jesus, My Prince Charming!

Worth the Wait

It is a privilege to have this time to share my heart with you. I want to encourage you in your walk of purity and let you know that if you wait for the man God has promised you, it will be worth the wait.

If you have compromised your purity, I am here to tell you that the blood of Christ covers your sin. Once you have repented, you can move forward, cleansed and pure once again. I have seen many a hurt young woman devastated by a relationship with a man where she gave herself sexually to him only to have him end the relationship.

This is not God's design for His daughters. His desire is for a young woman to wait until she is married to enjoy the sexual relationship; to experience the beauty of two people who love and are committed to each other becoming one flesh. When we give ourselves away prematurely, joining our flesh with that of someone outside the confines of marriage, there is a part of ourselves that we lose. It is painful and goes completely against what God has set aside to be something so very wonderful between a husband and a wife.

God is your heavenly Father and the rules He has for living are for your protection. In every boundary He has set up, He has your best interest in mind. Will you trust him and wait, knowing it will be worth it?

You are a treasured and valuable possession to God. A man who loves God will value your relationship with Him and he will refuse to do anything to hurt you spiritually. God wants your husband to love you like He loves you and to protect you like He protects you. A man that would interfere in your love relationship with God is not a man that is worth it.

One of my prayers for the message of "Truly Beautiful" is that a young woman would come to understand her value in Christ, and stay true to her resolve to stay pure. If you have lost your virginity, Jesus offers a second chance. He has forgiven you and asks that you merely confess, repent, and "go and sin no more".

Let's Talk About It

How are you doing in the area of your resolve to stay pure? What is your biggest struggle?

BEAUTY TRUTH #15 = to be truly beautiful is to live pure.

Apply it to Your Life

1. What precautions can you take as it relates to your resolve to remain pure?

2. What does the Bible teach about sexual purity? Record two or three verses that will be helpful to you in the future.

Pause and Pray

Making a decision ahead of time to remain pure is valuable in experiencing victory over sexual sin. Take a moment to pause and pray. Make a vow with God to live pure and ask Him to give you the strength to walk in purity. Sign the pledge below and share your commitment with someone who will encourage you to stay faithful to Jesus.

Believing that true love waits, I make a commitment to God, myself, my family, my friends, my future mate, and my future children to a lifetime of purity including sexual abstinence from this day until the day I enter a biblical marriage relationship.

Signed_____**Date**_____

Week 7

The Right Mirror

My Princess

Guard Your Mind

I want your mind fixed on Me, my beloved. But I want even more from you.

I desire great things for you, so I want you to guard your mind by making an "aware list" of all the things you watch, listen to, and read. Let me show you the things that can carry you away from your calling and destroy your dedication to Me. Even your thoughts can be held captive by the ways of the world. I want to protect you, but I will never force you to listen to My Spirit or make your mind dwell on what is true, pure, and right. The choice is yours, My love. You can have an abundant life, a blessed life, a life of influence for others to follow; or you can join the way of the world.

I, your God am asking you today to let your mind dwell on Me and you will discover the kind of life you long to enjoy, not only now, but forever.

Love,

Your King and your

Peace of Mind

Sheri Rose Shepherd

This Week's Focus

The Right Mirror

Read Ephesians 4:17-24.

This I say, therefore, and testify in the Lord, that you should no longer walk as the rest of the Gentiles walk, in the futility of their mind, having their understanding darkened, being alienated from the life of God, because of the ignorance that is in them, because of the blindness of their heart; who, being past feeling, have given themselves over to lewdness, to work all uncleanness with greediness. But you have not so learned Christ, if indeed you have heard Him and have been taught by Him, as the truth is in Jesus: that you put off, concerning your former conduct, the old man which grows corrupt according to the deceitful lusts, and be renewed in the spirit of your mind, and that you put on the new man which was created according to God, in true righteousness and holiness.

I think you would agree with me that in order to see ourselves we need a mirror. Imagine how ridiculous it would be to put on your make-up or style your hair without a mirror. You might attempt it and think you look okay but would you really want to risk it?

Spiritually, we don't want to risk it either. As women, one of our biggest problems are the mirrors we use, where and who we look to for a clearer understanding of who we are. You might recognize some of these mirrors we look into:

- The mirror of our peers
- The mirror of our parents
- The mirror of men
- The mirror of our past
- The mirror of public opinion

Typically, we look into the mirror of other people's opinions and a desire for their approval. Whether it is our appearance, our performance, or our status, we desire that approval. When you were a child, you looked into the mirror of your parent's opinion and depending on what you saw; you believed what they told you about yourself. We quickly see that these mirrors, whether our parents or someone else, often reflect an image that is not only one-sided, distorted and unreliable, but also very changeable. When other people's smiles of approval are replaced by frowns of disapproval, it can quickly lead to guilt, even hostility.

The ideal mirror is the Word of God's love and truth as He has revealed them in His Word. As a Christian young woman, you can open your Bible and find on its pages accurate insights into how God views you. His Word reveals His total forgiveness, His perfect and limitless love for you, His constant supply of strength, encouragement, and His exciting purposes for your life. These truths help you to cultivate the image of God in you. These truths never change. It's in God's Word that you can find reliable and uplifting truths about yourself. Dwelling on these truths can produce obedient, confident and joyful living.

BEAUTY TRUTH #16 – to be truly beautiful is to believe the only reliable mirror is the mirror of God's Word.

Apply it to Your Life

Mirror, mirror on the wall. We don't need a magic mirror to tell us how beautiful we are; the Bible is the only mirror we need. When we look into God's Word, He tells us exactly who we are and what we have in Him.

1. Gaze upon your beautiful reflection. Pick a **few** words from each of the following verses that help you to understand that you are ***truly beautiful***.

    -   Ephesians 1:4
    -   Ephesians 1:7-8
    -   Ephesians 2:4-5
    -   Ephesians 2:18
    -   Ephesians 3:12
    -   Colossians 1:14
    -   Colossians 1:27
    -   Colossians 2:7
    -   Colossians 2:10
    -   Colossians 2:12
    -   Colossians 2:13
    -   Colossians 3:1-4

2. What mirrors have you been looking into that have lied to you?

3. Why is it important that we look only into the mirror of God's Word?

4. Why is the mirror of other people's opinion unreliable?

5. There are **5** great truths that are ours to live out and embrace that the enemy will seek to tear down. Look up these truths in Scripture and write them out.

- Romans 6:6

- Galatians 5:16

- Ephesians 2:10

- Philippians 1:6

- 1 John 1:7

Let's Talk About It

Now that you have discovered the glorious truth of Scripture, which of these truths do you struggle to believe?

Week 8

The Right Wardrobe

Cleaning out the Closet

Yes, we are a new creation, but Scripture makes it clear that there is still a desire to return to the old life. We must constantly be recognizing and rejecting lies that come from our old self and our old way of living. It is not merely our old actions, but our old outlooks and attitudes that can creep in.

I am sure we can all relate to dirty laundry! We certainly don't want to walk in today what we wore yesterday. *Put off* means to take it off! Paul is using the simplest of terms to illustrate what we must do in the realm of our thought lives and attitudes. We must do this because in reality thoughts become attitudes and attitudes become actions. Putting off thoughts that reap havoc in our lives will spare us the attitudes and actions that will certainly follow. The same way we throw old clothes out of the closet that don't fit anymore; we throw off our old ways!

Put off the old. That is the first step. The other is to recognize the wonderful possibilities of the new life! If you think about the frustration of trying to change without the Spirit of God, it certainly is a hopeless situation.

But of all human beings, born again Christians have the possibility of doing something entirely different, living by an entirely different principle, because they have been renewed in the attitude of their minds. And that happens in the born again life as the Spirit of God comes into the heart that believes in Jesus Christ. When we believe in Jesus Christ and receive Him as our Lord and Savior, we are renewed in the attitudes of our minds. The new self is in the likeness of God; it is the life of God; it is the image of Jesus Christ; it is His life lived in you.

A New Wardrobe

If you are anything like me you have experienced one of those frustrating "I don't have anything to wear" moments. It may have been a prom or a birthday party or another special occasion that prompted you to try on everything in your closet, only to discover that you must have something "new". What's in the closet will just not work!

You might laugh but that is really what Ephesians chapter 4 is talking about. It carries the idea of putting off a set of clothes. Think of a prisoner who is released from prison, but still wearing his prison clothes, acting like a prisoner and not a free man. The first thing you would tell him is go put on some new clothes!

So it should be with our new lives in Christ. Anything other than Christ-like character and attitudes will not do! We have not so learned Christ, in other words, we know better. Just like putting on new clothes will change the way we think about ourselves and see ourselves, the same goes for putting on new attitudes and actions. This means that we shouldn't wait to feel like the new woman before we put on the new woman.

BEAUTY TRUTH #17 - to be truly beautiful is to put off the old self and put on the new self!

Apply it to Your Life

I need a new wardrobe!

1. Identify what you need to **put off** from your old life. Then, identify what you need to **put on** in order to walk in your new life.

   I will **put off** _____ and **put on** _____

   I will **put off** _____ and **put on** _____

   I will **put off** _____ and **put on** _____

   I will **put off** _____ and **put on** _____

   I will **put off** _____ and **put on** _____

2. Read Galatians 5:22-26. The fruits of the Spirit are a good way to measure if God's Word and His Holy Spirit are changing you. Are you growing in these fruits? Why or why not?

Your New Wardrobe

1. What new clothes will you add to your wardrobe from Colossians 3:12-17?

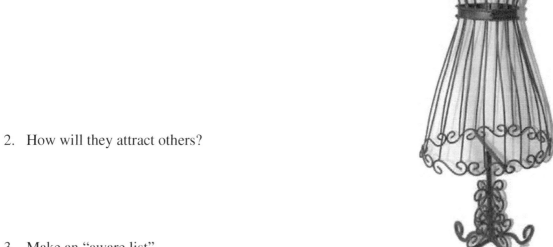

2. How will they attract others?

3. Make an "aware list".

    •   What movies are you watching?

    •   What songs are you listening to?

    •   What books are you reading?

    Which of these activities ***do not belong*** in your new wardrobe?

An Inside Job

So many of us want to make changes in our lives, but definitely go about it the wrong way. The word **transformed** used in Romans 12:2 is the Greek word, **metamorphoo**, which comes from metamorphosis. Picture the process of the transformation of a worm into a beautiful butterfly.

God's Word actually instructs us to be **morphed** or changed. This single word provides the key for understanding how spiritual transformation occurs. It directly challenges our ideas about trying harder to live holy lives. It emphasizes God's power and participation. Our way leads to frustration, failure and disappointment, but God's way leads to metamorphosis, a changed life. Just as God miraculously, supernaturally, turns a caterpillar into a beautiful butterfly, so He supernaturally transforms us into a new creation.

Transformation is not a switching from the to-do list of the flesh to the to-do list of the law. In Galatians 5, when Paul replaces the list of the works of the flesh, he does not replace it with the works of the law but the fruit of the Spirit! The Christian alternative to immoral behaviors is not a new list of moral behaviors. Instead of trying to be good we need to rely on and rest in God changing us. It is the triumphant power and transformation of the Holy Spirit through faith in Jesus Christ, and the supernatural power of the Word of God that changes us from the inside out!

Paul uses an amazing phrase in Ephesians 4:23 that parallels this thought. He says, "Be renewed in the spirit of your minds." Now what in the world is that? Our minds have a spirit, a bent, a mindset that is hostile to the absolute Lordship of Christ in our lives. This is where a young woman's selfish desire for beauty comes from. She sees herself more worthy of praise. She attributes her achievements to her own efforts. Her mindset is normally, it's all about me! The beauty battle begins in our minds. Because this is true, it is important that we change the way we think, so we can change the way we live.

BEAUTY TRUTH #18 = to be truly beautiful is to be transformed by the renewing of our mind.

Apply it to Your Life

1. Are you nourishing your mind with the truths of God's Word? Why or why not?

NO MORE STINKING THINKING!

2. Write out Romans 8:5-6.

3. What are some practical ways we can allow the Holy Spirit to control our minds?

4. Philippians 4:8 (NLT) teaches us what to think about in the list below. Beside each **<u>right</u>** thought, use an opposite word to describe a **<u>wrong</u>** thought.

RIGHT THINKING	WRONG THINKING
1. TRUE	1.
2. HONORABLE	2.
3. RIGHT	3.
4. PURE	4.
5. LOVELY	5.
6. ADMIRABLE	6.
7. EXCELLENT	7.
8. WORTHY OF PRAISE	8.

On a scale of 1-10, with 10 being right thinking and 0 being wrong thinking, how would you rate your thinking?

The Beauty of Holiness

It is frightening to think and altogether true that words like **discretion**, **holiness**, **modesty** and **purity** are disappearing from our world's vocabulary. In a culture that is rapidly declining morally, it is easy to become desensitized to the idea of walking in holiness and what it really means.

Holiness on a larger scale implies **faithfulness** – faithfulness to God and His Word. The new young woman in Christ is created in God's image, in true righteousness and holiness. Her *position* in Christ is to be worked out *practically* in her life.

Limiting the definition of holiness to certain areas of the Christian life actually does more harm than good. We want to embrace holiness as faithfulness to Christ. When we understand that the boundaries for living that God places in His Word are for our protection, we appreciate the quality of life that obedience to the Word of God brings.

Holiness is not something we do – it is what Jesus did for us. God sees you as holy, covered by the blood of Christ. But this truth should set you free to be who you really are and motivate you to live that way, set apart.

A set apart life is a truly beautiful life. It is a life that attracts others to it. A young woman who knows who she is in Christ, and walks in the fullness of that knowledge, radiates and communicates a beauty that is not seen in the world. The lure of that beauty is not fleshly, it is spiritual and it brings forth eternal fruit.

Whether it is the way we dress, the way we speak, the movies we choose to watch or waiting until we are married to have sex, it all comes from a heart that loves God and desires to be faithful to Him. It is a heart that is grateful and understands the high price that Jesus paid by going to the cross. It is a heart that values a redeemed life.

This is a heart that is engaged in relationship, not duty; a heart that so loves the One who has saved you, that you can do nothing else, but be faithful to Him and to live to please Him. This is the attitude of holiness. Have you ever had someone tell you they see Jesus in you? That is the greatest compliment you could ever hope to hear. It reveals that you are walking in the light and that the character traits that won people to Jesus are alive and well in you. Oh, how you need to be an example of light, so that your friends who are walking in darkness, can be won to Christ through you!

Holiness, holiness is what I long for
Holiness is what I need
Holiness, holiness is what You want from me

So, take my heart and form it
Take my mind and transform it
Take my will and conform it
To Yours, to Yours, oh, Lord

BEAUTY TRUTH #19 - to be truly beautiful is to live a lifestyle of holiness.

Apply it to Your Life

1. Look up the word **holiness** in a Bible dictionary and journal the definitions that help you to better understand it.

2. Why is it important to recognize that holiness should invade your entire life?

3. Write out the words of Psalm 29:2. What does it mean to worship the Lord in the beauty of holiness?

4. Have you discovered that God's boundaries for your life are there for your protection? Why or Why not?

5. What happens when you step out of those boundaries?

6. Find two or three Scriptures today that can help you as you seek to walk in an attitude of holiness.

Week 9

His Masterpiece

You Are My Masterpiece

_I_ love what I have created. _I_ am delighted in you!

Don't ever feel insecure about what you think you are not, because I made you in my image and your uniqueness is a gift from Me. I did not give you a life, My love, for you to squeeze into a man-made mold. You are royalty, but you won't discover that truth by gazing into a mirror. Let Me be your mirror and I will reflect back to you your true beauty. The more you gaze at Me, the more you will see my masterpiece in you. The sooner you see yourself for who you really are, the sooner you begin your reign as My priceless princess with a purpose.

Love,

Your King and your Creator

One of a Kind

God created each of us uniquely and we are "truly beautiful" just the way He made us. Psalm 139:13-16 tells us how we are to think about ourselves:

For You formed my inward parts; You covered me in my mother's womb. I will praise You, for I am fearfully and wonderfully made; Marvelous are Your works, and that my soul knows very well. My frame was not hidden from You, when I was made in secret, and skillfully wrought in the lowest parts of the earth. Your eyes saw my substance, being yet unformed. And in Your book they all were written, the days fashioned for me, when as yet there were none of them.

Each of us is irreplaceable, one of a kind, priceless! And sometimes I wonder if it isn't like a slap in God's face when we are disappointed in who He made us to be or wanting to be someone else. In C.S. Lewis', Voyage of the Dawntreader, Lucy has discovered the Book of Incantations. A green mist forms behind her as she begins to read:

An infallible spell to make you she –the beauty you've always wanted to be.

The book becomes a mirror and in the mirror she sees her sister Susan's reflection. Realizing the spell has turned her into her sister, she says, "I'm beautiful." Lucy's desire is temporarily granted and she quickly finds herself in a world without Lucy. She begins to panic as pieces of her life begin to disappear. Aslan enters the scene and asks,

"What have you done, child?
You wished yourself away and with it much more."

How about you, are you wishing yourself away? We can be just like Lucy, tempted to want to be someone else, longing for their life instead of our own. Think about that seriously for a moment. Who in your world is looking to you to lead the way? If you decided to be someone else who would miss out on what your life brings?

In our worst moments, we wonder about our purpose, our value, and our significance. In those moments, let's look at the beautiful universe God has created and then push back the voice of Satan who is trying to make us feel valueless and hear the voice of God, "You are my masterpiece, created to bring a blessing to others."

God has an amazing plan and purpose for **your life**, that no one else can fulfill but you. He has uniquely gifted you for what it is that He has created you to do! When you begin to walk in the works that He has planned for you, when you begin to embrace the way He has made you, you will discover a passion for life that you never had before!

BEAUTY TRUTH #20 = to be truly beautiful is to know your value. You are God's masterpiece.

Apply it to Your Life

1. Masterpiece has been defined as the greatest work of an artist and you are God's greatest work. Do you think of yourself as God's greatest work? Why or why not?

2. Think of the most spectacular sunset setting against the backdrop of God's vast ocean and know this creation was not His ultimate workmanship, you are! Read Romans 12:3. How are we told to see ourselves?

3. Is your opinion of yourself too high or too low? Explain.

4. Paste a few pictures below that reveal something about who God made you to be; consider your personality, your hobbies, your friends and family, your hopes and dreams!

5. Take some time to read and meditate upon the truths presented below. Journal your thoughts when you are done reading.

In Christ you are of untold worth. You may have had things happen which make you doubt your worth. But you are His workmanship, His work of art, moreover you are in process.

Michelangelo was once asked what he was doing as he chipped away at a shapeless work. He replied, "I am liberating an angel from this stone." That's what God is doing with you. You are in the hands of the Great Maker, the ultimate Sculptor who created the universe out of nothing, and He has never yet thrown away a rock on which He has begun a masterwork. But even though you are in process, you must have faith to trust in what God already sees! He will be faithful to complete His work in you. He is already doing that now through His Word and His Holy Spirit. Everything that happens to you is another beautiful brush on the canvas, not one stroke is out of place.

Remember, you are God's special treasure, selected by Him and for Him. You are created in the image of Almighty God. He made you exactly the way He intended, and He equipped you with everything you need. You have the strength to stand strong in the midst of difficult situations and the wisdom it takes to make good decisions. Understanding exactly whose you are, and how you fit in God's plan creates purpose, confidence and identity. You have an assignment and you are full of gifts, talents, encouragement and love. You have rich treasure inside you that people need. You have the power of Christ living in you to accomplish more than you ever thought possible. Dare to be bold in your calling, because the time grows short.

Journal your thoughts

A Life of Significance

In a conversation from Alice in Wonderland, Alice asks the Cheshire cat, "Would you tell me, please, which way I ought to go from here?"

"That depends a good deal on where you want to get to," said the Cat. "I don't much care where," said Alice. "Then it doesn't matter which way you go," said the Cat.

Our lives are not to be aimless. God has a plan and purpose for your life that only you can fulfill. Christ-likeness and Christ's glory gives purpose to every believer's life. God's Word teaches us how to live like Christ. As we begin to resemble Christ, we become aware of how He made us; we begin to discover the gifts He has given us to bring Him glory. As we understand and receive His love, we are then able to share it in the spheres of influence where He has placed us.

As we discover how He has made us, and the gifts He has blessed us, with we are able to bring a focus to our lives. His unique purpose for us will determine how we spend our time, energy and resources. When we discover what we were made to do, we will wake up every morning eager and excited to play a part in His kingdom plan. What God has created us to do, we love to do and we never grow weary of doing it.

As you begin to walk in the purpose and plan that God has for your life, He will be faithful to lead you. If your heart's desire is to bring Him glory and if you yield to His perfect plan, you will live a life of eternal significance. Your desire to make a difference in the world will be fulfilled when you step into God's plan and purpose for you.

BEAUTY TRUTH #21 = to be truly beautiful is to walk in the purpose and plan that God has for your life.

Apply it to Your Life

1. Read 1 Corinthians 12:1-11 and Romans 12:3-8. List the spiritual gifts that God gives to believers.

2. There are three reasons why it is important to know your spiritual gifts:

   - Knowing your spiritual gifts will enable you to find your place of ministry in the local church.
   - Knowing your spiritual gifts will enable you to determine your priorities.
   - Knowing your spiritual gifts will be of great help in discerning God's will.

Pause and Pray.

Ask God to reveal your spiritual gifts as you take the spiritual gift test below.

Assessing Your Spiritual Gifts (Thank you to Debbi Bryson @ www.biblebusstop.com)

"To each one the manifestation of the Spirit is given for the common good."
1 Corinthians 12:7

Administration
- ❑ I like to organize events, information and people
- ❑ I anticipate potential problems and find a solution
- ❑ I pay attention to details
- ❑ I set a plan in place, but can flex when needed

Encouragement
- ❑ I often see strengths in others that they may not recognize
- ❑ **I notice those who are not included**
- ❑ It is easy for me to verbalize encouragement—and others receive it

Mercy
- ❑ When others fail, I desire to restore
- ❑ I notice those who are broken or weak
- ❑ I easily spot pain, and easily empathize

Discernment
- ❑ I often feel a *check* about whether a situation is good or bad
- ❑ I often sense underlying motives
- ❑ I sometimes am correctly aware of hidden sin before it is confessed or revealed

Counseling
- ❑ I am a good listener, others feel comfortable and safe sharing
- ❑ I am careful with confidences
- ❑ I am prompted to seek the underlying causes to problems
- ❑ Biblical wisdom and a restored relationship with God is my highest goal

Faith
- ❑ To me, the problem always appears smaller than God
- ❑ I am constantly aware of God's capabilities and resources
- ❑ Once I know the will of God, circumstances are immaterial
- ❑ I have many fresh testimonies of God's faithfulness

Helps

- ❑ I would rather take on practical tasks than lead
- ❑ I like working behind the scenes
- ❑ I am aware of material needs but also know the spiritual reason for the ministry I serve

Hospitality

- ❑ I love to make people comfortable
- ❑ No one feels unwelcome in my presence
- ❑ I seek to show and make God's love tangible with food or shelter as needed

Teaching

- ❑ I love the Bible and am constantly drawn to read and study for myself
- ❑ I am thrilled when I can help others understand and apply God's truths
- ❑ Understanding the context and background of scripture is important. Accuracy is vital
- ❑ I value and learn from gifted Bible teachers - I am teachable

Exhortation

- ❑ Obedience to God is a personal passion
- ❑ Speaking the truth with love seems simple, if not always easy
- ❑ I am not afraid of challenging others to high standards

Word of Wisdom

- ❑ Often, I can see a profoundly simple solution in the midst of a difficult situation
- ❑ Wise words come in situations that could be volatile or divisive
- ❑ Sometimes I am aware of an answer to an unspoken question

Pastoring, Shepherding

- ❑ I take a long term interest in nurturing and caring for people's spiritual needs
- ❑ Instead of developing a dependency on me, I teach them to rely on Jesus
- ❑ Helping bear others burdens brings me joy
- ❑ I teach others to feed themselves and grow

Evangelism

- ❑ I have a constant—heartfelt burden for the lost
- ❑ I feel comfortable speaking of spiritual truths and needs with non-Christians
- ❑ The Gospel truth of the cross is a joy to share

Leadership

- ❑ Others follow
- ❑ Others learn to grow and take on responsibility and ownership of the ministry
- ❑ Diligence is a pleasure

Ministering

- ❑ One on one personal ministry is of special interest
- ❑ Others come to me for prayer needs
- ❑ I allow others to grieve
- ❑ I know when to speak and when to be silent, just listening

Be aware that often several complimentary gifts are given together. According to the needs and situation, some gifts might be inactive. At others times they are freely manifested. Let the Spirit lead and minister through you. Even when you become familiar with a gift in operation in your life, never take it for granted. Keep your dependency fresh. Keep your vessel clean. Keep your motives pure. Keep the fires of your love for Jesus strong. Never love the gifts more than the Giver.

Summarize what you discovered after assessing your spiritual gifts

God Confidence

Are you surprised to learn that some of the great leaders in Scripture struggled with the same feelings of inadequacy that you do? I am certainly encouraged to know that I am not alone in believing I can't do something. What is the real problem with this kind of thinking? I am looking at myself and comparing myself to the task to which God has called me. No wonder I feel inadequate. *I am inadequate*.

Yet God does not call me to do anything for Him out of my own resources. He calls me to be faithful and to allow Him to work through me. This involves stepping out in faith. It is scary because God doesn't show me His entire plan or the outcome.

We see Moses' reluctance to answer the call of God, yet this is the same man who stood before Pharaoh and who led the children of Israel as they crossed the Red Sea. Just as God gave Moses what he needed to be the leader and the deliverer of the children of Israel, we have been given what we need to accomplish the task God has assigned us to.

Paul said that he "put no confidence in the flesh" (Philippians 3:3). In other words, he didn't think that he was good enough because of any particular talent or ability that he had on his own. But his confidence came from his understanding of who he was as a child of God. Someone once said, "A man wrapped up in himself makes a pretty small package. But a man, or woman, wrapped up in God is an amazing sight to behold."

Confidence in God empowers us, energizes us, and strengthens us. It is this confidence in God that is going to make it possible to achieve and accomplish anything and everything that God the Father sets out before us. Confidence in God drives out fear, doubt, anxiety, and worry, allowing us to make an impact in the world for Him.

God confidence believes that I am His masterpiece! He has created me for a purpose and plan that has eternal implications. He will supply all that I need to walk forward in that calling, but I must have faith to take the first step!

BEAUTY TRUTH #21 – to be truly beautiful is to be **<u>GOD</u>** confident!

Apply it to Your Life

Moses had asked, "Who am I?" implying his complete **inadequacy** *for his calling. In Exodus 3:14 God replied, "I am who I am!" implying His complete* **adequacy**. *The issue was not who Moses was but who God is.*

1. Can you identify with Moses and with his feelings of inadequacy? What are some areas in which God might want to use you, but you may be holding back due to fear?

2. Read Jeremiah 1:4-8. How did Jeremiah feel when God called him to be a prophet? What were his hesitations? How did God answer him?

3. What is the difference between self-confidence and God-confidence? Why is this important?

4. Perhaps you are reluctant to follow God. How do the following verses encourage you to be **God**-confident?

   - Philippians 1:6

   - Philippians 3:4-9

   - Philippians 4:13

   - 2 Timothy 1:7

Pause and Pray

If you struggle with feeling inadequate, confess to the Lord that you are focusing on yourself and your resources instead of on Him and His resources. Write a prayer asking God to help you remember to choose to be God-confident instead of self-confident. Thank Him for being the all-sufficient God!

Dear Jesus,

Week 10

Living as His Masterpiece

In Review

Living as God's masterpiece will mean cementing the 21 beauty truths of "Truly Beautiful" in your heart and mind. Go back to your study and write out all 21 beauty truths below.

BEAUTY TRUTH #1 =

BEAUTY TRUTH #2 =

BEAUTY TRUTH #3 =

BEAUTY TRUTH #4 =

BEAUTY TRUTH #5 =

BEAUTY TRUTH #6 =

BEAUTY TRUTH #7 =

BEAUTY TRUTH #8 =

BEAUTY TRUTH #9 =

BEAUTY TRUTH #10 =

BEAUTY TRUTH #11 =

BEAUTY TRUTH #12 =

BEAUTY TRUTH #13 =

BEAUTY TRUTH #14 =

BEAUTY TRUTH #15 =

BEAUTY TRUTH #16 =

BEAUTY TRUTH #17 =

BEAUTY TRUTH #18 =

BEAUTY TRUTH #19 =

BEAUTY TRUTH #20 =

BEAUTY TRUTH #21 =

1. Go back and circle your favorite three beauty truths. Explain why they are your favorite.

2. Put a big star by the beauty truth that most changed the way you think. How will you go about putting this truth into action?

3. Now that you have completed the study, what do you think God wants you to do next?

4. We have a great God! Share a God-sized dream and don't be afraid to believe God for it! Have your friends join you in prayer! If your heart and motive is to bring God glory, He can make it happen!

How has the study of Truly Beautiful changed your life?

*In your pursuit of the abundant life in Christ, don't ever forget who you are in Him. Renew your mind continually to the truths below, and know that you are **TRULY BEAUTIFUL!***

Who I Am In Christ

I am accepted

I am God's child - John 1:12
As a disciple, I am a friend of Jesus Christ - John 15:15
I have been justified - Romans 5:1
I am united with the Lord and I am one with Him in Spirit - 1 Corinthians 6:17
I have been bought with a price and I belong to God - 1 Corinthians 6:19-20
I am a member of Christ's body - 1 Corinthians 12:27
I have been chosen by God and adopted as His child - Ephesians 1:3-8
I have been redeemed and forgiven of all my sins - Colossians 1:13-14
I am complete in Christ - Colossians 2:9-10
I have direct access to the throne of grace through Jesus Christ - Hebrews 4:14-16

I am secure

I am free from condemnation - Romans 8:1-2
I am assured God works for my good in all circumstances - Romans 8:28
I am free from any condemnation brought against me and
I cannot be separated from the love of God - Romans 8:31-39
I have been established, anointed and sealed by God - 2 Corinthians 1:21-22
I am hidden with Christ in God - Colossians 3:1-4
I am confident that God will complete the good work He started in me - Philippians 1:6
I am a citizen of heaven - Philippians 3:20
I have not been given a spirit of fear but of power, love and a sound mind - 2 Timothy 1:7
I am born of God and the evil one cannot touch me - 1 John 5:18

I am significant

I am a branch of Jesus Christ, the true vine, and a channel of His life - John 15:5
I have been chosen and appointed to bear fruit - John 15:16
I am God's temple - 1 Corinthians 3:16
I am a minister of reconciliation for God - 2 Corinthians 5:17-21
I am seated with Jesus Christ in the heavenly realm - Ephesians 2:6
I am God's workmanship - Ephesians 2:10
I may approach God with freedom and confidence - Ephesians 3:12
I can do all things through Christ who strengthens me - Philippians 4:13

About the Author

Margy Hill's passion and calling for women's ministry led her to start the Women's Ministry Connection where she encourages and exhorts women leaders in ministry. God has given her the opportunity to speak into the lives of women of all ages and church backgrounds.

She loves to teach and share her passion for the Word of God to stir women to a deeper and more abundant relationship with Jesus and to encourage and equip them to walk in the fullness of their callings.

Her gift for writing has led her to write several Bible studies to help women develop a desire to dig deeper into the Word of God. With challenging questions and everyday application, her studies have been widely used throughout churches in the United States.

Margy speaks and teaches for women's conferences, retreats and seminars and is also known for her "Hope for the Hurting Heart" training workshops to help equip women to counsel confidently from the Word of God.

Margy resides in Newport News, Virginia and is blessed to be able to serve with her husband who is the "Reaching Around" Pastor at Calvary Chapel Newport News. She loves being a part of the women's ministry team, serving the women in weekly Bible study.

For more information, visit her website at www.wmconnection.org